YEARS GREW A KELOID

ASH GOOD

Copyright © 2014 by Ash Good.
Portland, Ore.

With gratitude to Dr. Karen Mary Davalos and Karen Kevorkian for their encouragement during the creation of the original version of this work. And also Michael Ventura and Jazmin Aminian Jordán for their time, keen insight and wise guidance. And also my mama who deserves more thanks than I can ever possibly give.

All rights reserved. No part of this book may be reproduced, stored in, or introduced into a retrieval system, or transmitted, in any form or by any means (electronic, mechanical, photocopying, recording or otherwise) without the written permission of the author.

ISBN 978-0-9972987-0-3
Ebook ISBN 978-0-9972987-1-0

"When you write an advice columnist about your daddy issues" on page 24 includes a response written by the anonymous blogger The Coquette. The original exchange can be found online at http://dearcoquette.com/on-biological-fatherlessness/. Reprinted with permission.

Names and locations in this work may resemble real persons or places, but these stories are solely the product of the author's (faulty) memory and best regarded as fanciful fact.

Cover illustration by Momo Juniper Hurley.

This book was typeset in MrsEaves with headers in Biko and Montserrat.

ASHGOOD.COM

For each of you who've reflected truth.
And, hell,
even for those who've reflected lies.

WORDS

Crying in a dandelion field 11

The soil where you're planted 12

Great Grandma Rose and the very tiny spoon 13

D.A.R.E. 15

In their big mirror. 17

You didn't listen when your eighth grade algebra teacher pleaded:

    don't get married until you're 25 19

Stillness 22

When you write an advice columnist about your daddy issues . . . 24

Really bad at bicycles 29

In Inglechester 34

Because, goddamnit. 36

Drugs are dangerous kids / you'll never be the same 38

Okay, cupid 42

We cannot be more sensitive to pleasure without being more sensitive to pain.

—Alan Watts

CRYING IN A DANDELION FIELD

YOU KNEW YOURSELF from the photos
in that hefty peach velour album
tucked in the avalanche closet

Some other time where you learned
(and then forgot) that it's a long drive
from Corning, California, to Juneau, Alaska,
strapped in a car seat in a blue Chevy Luv

When the world was small and you wore a striped
tank-top and toddler pretty-panties and
drowned in daddy's Budweiser trucker hat
and teethed on gramp's frosty beer mug

When you were all blunt heavy bangs
hanging over squinty eyes
sunk in a pink puffy face
neon t-shirt, shorts on chubby legs

The trip to the water park where a diaper wearing chimp
sat between you and mama and daddy and Jeffy,
cheeks flush from sunshine and smiles

In your favorite memory that you don't have
you're sitting in a field of yellow dandelions
and have nothing but tears
for your mama's Kodak film

THE SOIL WHERE YOU'RE PLANTED

THERE IS ALWAYS a hydrangea
front right flower bed next to the gate
consumed by Morning Glory
a woman comes to the garage sale and says
That sure is an unusual color for a hydrangea
then her and gran talk about the weather
you like to think
that your hydrangea
is rare

GREAT GRANDMA ROSE AND THE VERY TINY SPOON

GREAT GRANDMA ROSE is the matriarch of a curious
bunch. She lives in a white clap-board house
in the middle of town, straight across from the Grace Baptist
Church (where she faithfully attends every Sunday
with her youngest-though-near-elderly son, a most loving
lad who had fallen on his head).

In the front room of her house
(that smells a little strange if you honestly admit)
she rocks in her chair
while her knotty, white knuckles knit.
The television is at a constant rumble, tuned in
on an antennae. In the next room the built-in buffet
drawers brim with neatly aligned teensy, tiny spoons
brought to the stooping, silver-haired centenarian
by her great-grandchildren and grandchildren and children
and church-going friends.

How often folks would proudly return from near and far
to present Great Grandma Rose with a new addition
to her large assembly of tiny utensils!

When your daddy jets off to Puerto Vallarta (for
a week in the sun drinking Corona with Cousin Don)
he brings back an Inca-inspired very tiny spoon.
You fondly admire that gift in the vast collection
knowing it is from your daddy's adventures
(and thus the smallest, teensiest bit from you).

When Great Grandma Rose passes, to be most fair,
each entry to the very large teensy, tiny spoon collection
is returned to its original giver.

So that exotic specimen of your fancy—
a green block of jade handle carved in sharp tiki relief
with perfect round silver spoon off the end—
sits lonely on your kitchen table on the day
of her funeral (when you get home from riding bikes).

The travel trinket lacks its luster—homesick
for the grand array of its former company.
You suspiciously eye fairness for the first time
as the potential and formidable foe
of greatness.

D.A.R.E.

THERE ARE DAYS when Drug Dealer Steve
sits across the street on Yarmer Lane,
his shitty sedan facing your little green house.

He wears white tennis shoes and ill fitting,
faded pleat-front-slacks.
He stops at the gate a few steps from the porch
and with all his kindness muster-able
asks you (pudgy and eleven years)
Hey—is your dad around?

You size him up with the indignant glare
of a D.A.R.E. graduate (who weathers each
minute of the *Say No to Drugs* hoopla praying
that Officer Beasley won't know
that when he is berating drug using criminals
he is talking about your fireman dad).

Drug Dealer Steve drops his friendly tone:
He owes me money.

It is warm outside but
your hands start to shake.

*Maybe if you weren't a drug dealer,
no one would owe you money.*

Drug Dealer Steve doesn't expect
his collection efforts to end
in a dressing down from a child.
He steps back and stammers.

*Maybe if your dad
didn't do drugs
he wouldn't owe me any money.*

IN THEIR BIG MIRROR

CROCHETED THROWS on the daveneau
TV trays stacked by the kitchen jamb
Big Mouth Billy Bass
white paper with unsteady hand
smattering of stickers, topsy turvy
a child's love notes
Scotch-taped behind the rocking chair

faded frond print runs comfortable
under their big mirror

in their big mirror you're six and the
cubic zirconia studs don't sparkle like your grin
I'll pay ya sis if you get your ears pierced
maybe gramp bets you because he doesn't think you will
or he knows you can't back down from a challenge
but it works and now
you're surely almost grown-up

in their big mirror
you're eight, ruddy cheeked
fresh from catching snow
wearing gran's pretty old handkerchief
knotted at your chin
instead of a stocking cap

in their big mirror
it's the first stop on the trick-or-treat trail
you're a cowgirl
you're a cheerleader
you're a cat
you're a clown
you're a teenager

time and garage sales change
that pile of toys in the corner and
the design on the TV trays

in their big mirror
you're wise and old and twenty-eight
lessons learned in a new line between your brows
All I've figured out is that I don't know anything
he laughs and says *I hear ya, sis*

he tells you a story then
about buying that old aluminum boat on credit
It took gran and I damn near a coon's age to pay that sucker off
you remember this when
you buy a sensible wagon named Old Blue
and pen your name on the pink-slip after
handing the man a small pile of cash

YOU DIDN'T LISTEN WHEN YOUR EIGHTH GRADE ALGEBRA TEACHER PLEADED: DON'T GET MARRIED UNTIL YOU'RE 25

AT YOUR FIRST APPOINTMENT your husband looks trim but frazzled in his flat-front khakis (you picked out) and a lavender button-down (your favorite). He is on lunch. You meet him in the parking lot feeling like a child wearing your parents' clothes.

The waiting room is Asian-themed with Japanese prints. The therapist is a respectful-looking baby boomer. Zen Doctor Neil slouches informally and tries to understand your problem. What *is* the problem?
Perhaps your next two appointments you should each take alone.

At your second appointment (solo) Zen Doctor Neil picks up a marker, draws two lines and then looks expectantly between you and his simple whiteboard doodle.
It's going along great and both lines line up nicely
and then a point is reached where the slope of this line continues,
and this other line starts along a different path, and the two lines
stray further and further.

At your third appointment Zen Doctor Neil
talks about your inner child.
Pretend she's sitting right there in that chair.

At your fourth appointment, Zen Doctor Neil
says you look rushed and scattered. He hits a gong.
Focus on the sound.

At your fifth appointment, Zen Doctor Neil
reports that you will likely be surprised at
how much greater of a reaction you will compel
from men after losing another ten pounds.
When you walk into a room your intense and exuding
sexual energy affects people.

By your sixth appointment you look forward
to forking over the twenty dollar copay for the opportunity
to mentally fuck with this strange man
who has ended your marriage for you.
Let's talk about how you're an Adult Child of an Alcoholic.

At your seventh appointment Zen Doctor Neil seems confused.
Why are you here?

By appointment eight insurance coverage ends.

The fresh slice of divorce swiftly and expertly cut.
Numb then—barely tingled—but
years grew a keloid.

STILLNESS

> *The moment I'm alone, my deepest joy is to be nobody...*
> *there's no longer any sense of external identity. I simply go into the stillness more deeply.*
> *The place that I love most is the stillness. It's not that the stillness is lost...*
> *but when people leave me, there is only the stillness left. And I love that so much.*
> —Eckhart Tolle

YOU ARRIVE HOME from spending all day out there,
only eager to throw your bag in a chair,
exhaustedly fling yourself after it and,
over the course of a long sigh,
shed the heavy exterior you've held far too long.

And then, free from the labels
and the should be's and the trying to be's
and the smiles and the nods of agreement,
you wrestle with the subtle guilt of interacting
beneath such an intensely crafted self.
Of course this is no fault of theirs or yours.
All wily selves assemble roles to play.

You yearn for the stillness that comes after the sigh,
when the selves vanish and the curtain falls on the act.
But when it becomes still (and lonely),
you watch yourself scramble and cling.
Engage an instant message, a long distance phone call,
a flurry of texts; any shitty excuse
to keep the loathed charade going.

You want to be okay with the stillness.
So much so that you tell yourself and others that you are.
Even that you love it.
But in the stillness the only thing that is left to do
is sit in awe of the unmitigated power of the
life-force within you—the power within every human—
which is terrifying.

WHEN YOU WRITE AN ADVICE COLUMNIST ABOUT YOUR DADDY ISSUES

DEAR COQUETTE,

While you're on the subject of fatherlessness, I woke up from a dream today clear that I had a question for you. The details of the dream are, I suspect, unimportant, but the image that lingers is of me finding an old box that I keep under my bed as a kid. Inside is a tiny wallet-sized photo of my biological father. It is the one my mom gives me when I am about six, and instructs me to hide from the only person I ever know as my dad.

So in this dream, there's the portrait, just like I remember, and then facing it there's another picture—one I haven't seen before. The guy from the portrait is holding the baby version of me above him, smiling, our noses almost touching. That saccharine quality is enough to make me gag a little upon waking.

I find him on Facebook—my biological father. The internet is a funny place where a swift mouse click is the only thing separating you from communicating with a person you don't know but to whom you are innately and permanently connected. He's there. Along with his family.
I have a half-brother. A half-sister.

There's the grown up in me that doesn't want to fuck with something that isn't broken. My life is pretty damn good. It seems his is too. There are plenty of people who care about me deeply and I have the dad I grew up with (and I'm still afraid of hurting his feelings). But then there's a bratty child in me who wants to kick and scream and demand that this person acknowledge my existence. What do I do?

Find a private moment when you have a clear mind and an open heart. Sit down and write your biological father a letter. No other direction than that. Just sit and write. See what comes out. Find out what you have to say to him.

Get it out on the page, and then let it sit for a while. Walk away from it. Come back a week or a month later and revisit it. Check how you feel against how you felt. Write more if you need.

Over time, use what you learn about your emotions to inform your decision about how to proceed. Process as much as you can before taking any action.

Life is long, sweetheart. Whether it's a year from now or a decade, I have no doubt you'll eventually make some sort of contact with your biological father. Know yourself as much as possible before you do.

—The Coquette

✳ ✳ ✳

THINGS YOU MAY OR MAY NOT SAY TO YOUR BIOLOGICAL FATHER
- It's kind of funny how you get the multi-syllabic title that sounds scientifically official and honorific when the other guy gets such a short name that came with so much shit to deal with. I'll always call *him* dad.
- My mama feels immense shame about taking me so far from you. She confessed it to me tearfully once, driving in the car, when I was about eight. It was almost as awkward as the time she felt like a car-talk about menstruation was necessary since we were going to go buy clean little trashcans for the softball field ladies' restroom stalls.
- I don't know whether you even cared that she took me.
- Did you care?
- I already thought about whether or not I can take the proverbial punch in the stomach if the answer is no.
- It might be worse if it is yes.
- Did you wonder?
- Did you really ask her if I was yours?
- I hid what looked like a senior high school portrait of you in my jewelry box. I knew your name. I loved you like a TV star I'd never meet.
- I fantasized that you'd be at my high school graduation, proud as fuck. I don't know why I wished that. Probably because mama's-best-friend's-daughter had a story kinda like mine (though she is prett*ier* and more togeth*er* and all the *-ers*). Her California Dad showed up at her graduation. I guess all dreams come from somewhere.

- I did all that shit I was supposed to do to make you proud as fuck, just FYI. Straight A's. Pretty close to a full ride from my top choice school. Valedictorian speech and everything.
- You made the right decision, letting my dad adopt me.
- My family is shaped by decades of addiction. That means the love is real, but we love each other so much it hurts.
- I'm sorry the real you has to live on the same planet as my mythic imagination about you.
- I know we don't really have anything to do with one another but you're still there and I'm still here so there's still this *this*.
- I Face-stalked you.
- And then I judged you for loving *Burn Notice* and turkey hunting.
- I wrote an online advice columnist after a dream I had about you. Her advice was spot on.
- I don't want to meet you.
- I really want to meet you.
- I actually might not be able to take the proverbial punch in the stomach after all.
- I feel like I'm missing out not knowing my half-siblings.
- Fuck you.
- I love you.
- Where do you see you in me?
- I see me right there in you.

REALLY BAD AT BICYCLES

YOU GREW UP ON A FARM strewn across a down-sloping hill. No pavement. No flat surfaces. No cul-de-sacs. But santa brought a bike anyhow one year—handle bar streamers, training wheels and all. On maybe five or six occasions your mama lugged you and Jeffy and your two santa bikes over to Campbell Park and unloaded the whole sorry lot into the fenced-in tennis courts. You rode in circles on training wheels until the day you learned—with much shrieking, crashing and determination—to pedal on two wheels. Aunt Con took you back to the courts for the last time (on the day when you and Jeffy weren't old enough to go to Great Grandma Rose's funeral).

When you were a little bit bigger your mama took you and that old santa bike into town to play with Breezy. You and Breezy peddled all over lazy neighborhood streets. At the end of the ride you came flying like a bat-outta-hell into the driveway, planting your bike firmly into the rear-end of Breezy's mama's Civic. Your stomach dropped and you begged Breezy to the ends of the earth not to tattle about the obvious penny-sized crack in the tail-light.

When you were eleven, Josie and Joe wanted to ride bikes on day two of a four-day-pre-teen-slumber-party-bender so mama brought down that old bike. Josie and Joe confidently pedaled their 12-speed mountain bikes for miles and miles on the hills of Old Portland Road while you huffed and puffed and tried to keep up on the same old bike that had no gears and streamered handle bars and offered the support of training wheels a good many years before.

※ ※ ※

Now a svelte, red, vintage road bike sits in your living room, acquired from a downtown loft-living bicycle courier who lovingly built it for his lady-friend (you don't ask whether they broke up or the girl just didn't like it). Though smitten with the silhouette and character of this Craigslist-procured machine, you admittedly like it better when it isn't moving.

One particular day, wholly absorbed in avoiding collision with a bush, an upcoming chain link fence and an eight-inch ledge while you pedal the uncomfortable, bi-wheeled thing, your concentration is broken by a wiry man standing to the left of the sidewalk who loudly mutters *FATASS*.

Even though a decade has passed since you were legitimately fat, you inhabit, instantly, your obese teenage body again, trapped by menacing thought-energy of jiggly thighs and stocky calves as you awkwardly try to make that beautiful bike just. Fucking. Move. Away from him. Away from there. Anywhere but here.

Don't take anything personally. Agreement number 3.
Thanks Don Miguel Ruiz.

It's all a dream. If you get something from someone,
it's because of something you gave. Oh so helpful Osho.

Your tummy is pooching. Love you too, mama.

Tears but you refuse to let them fall.
An angry, fat, little girl screams with every pedal:

MY BODY ISN'T FUCKING FOR YOU.

My body isn't for you—who tries to tell me that it is too big when I am small and that it is too small now that I am big. It's not fucking for you.

My body isn't for you—who gives me that disapproving glance when I just need to hear I am beautiful in the dress I am wearing to Winterball and now tells me I'm beautiful every chance you get. Do you realize the cost of dragging those petty words from your mouth was literally erasing half of myself?

My body isn't for you—the stranger outside the Goodwill who huffs damn girl you have a sexy walk while you pretend I'm walking to your bed.

My body isn't for you—who runs your hands down this shape and tells me that my pussy and I are goddamn beautiful and then wants me to leave at three a.m.

My body isn't for you—who laughs about telling some friend you're trying to impress that it's okay that I'm not super-smokin-hot, because, you know, I'm a really great cook.

My body isn't for you—who mindlessly rants about repulsing large breasts even though you were touching mine earlier today.

My body isn't for you—who asks more than once if I have kids I didn't tell you about because you're confused by stretch marks on this soft belly of mine.

My body isn't for you—who tells me I'd get more ladyhead if I'd just shave down there.

My body isn't for you—who confesses that you were just so damn mad that you made me blow you last night even though I was blacked out.

And my body isn't for you—skinny man who wants to judge the size of my ass.

You fantasize about running the dude over on the way home. On accident. After all, you are pretty fucking terrible at riding bicycles.

When the tears finally come,
you hug that little girl and you whisper:

This body is for
        feeling the sun on your face and dandelions under your feet.
This body is for balancing in baksana like a goddamn ninja.
This body is for believing that intention can heal.
This body is for dancing.
This body is for feeling this miraculous place is so much
        more mysterious and magical than it is allowed to be.
With this body you'll know faeries and trolls and gnomes and
        plants that speak and dimensions that mingle
        and the energy that pours palpably from your being.
Love and nurture
        and forget the rest.

This body is for you. And it can ride a bicycle just fine.

IN INGLECHESTER

A WALK TO RANDY'S DONUTS—crossing the freeway overpass with no sidewalk (praying you won't have to talk your way out of a pedestrian citation from the prowling LAPD)—is best done past midnight, quickly and stealthily in the name of a hot-from-the-fryer buttermilk bar. When the world feels shifty, it can be set right by LA's best-known B-roll movie prop—the thirty-two-and-one-fifth-feet tall plaster donut at Manchester and the 405.

In Inglechester the best sunsets happen in the cracked vacant lot behind the dried-up Vons where there are always donut-shaped burnouts and shadows of abandoned shopping carts fall long. The same parking lot where you lay flat on your back to meditate mid-night touching the asphalt crust of the earth. The same parking lot where you learn how to ride a motorcycle and meet in clandestine style to make friends with an undercover Hasidic law student in the midst of an identity crisis.

In Inglechester afterhours you can sit outside the discount carpet and flooring store (with free in-house design) and puff a joint while the outdoor loudspeaker robustly proclaims the truths of Jesucristo, nuestro Señor y salvador. You walk past the dirty Baskin Robbins and the Magic Johnson's TGIFridays to the Goodwill where you buy a full spectrum of men's silk dress shirts, oversized cashmere sweaters and long house dresses donated by the wealthy residents of the bordering Black Beverly Hills.

In Inglechester you feel scared on the street only three times: When a Haitian enchantress who is shitting in the alley hexes you with a dark charm as you stroll by. When a man with riotous eyes and a suitcase stumbles in front of the stoop and menaces you on the sidewalk for six blocks. When you walk to the market hand-in-hand-in-hand, you and Sean and David one day. Real cute spit from the lips of a passer-by.

BECAUSE, GODDAMNIT

STUPID BITCHES say you have really good energy
in-eloquence for the presence of one who gives another
a g o d d a m n m i n u t e that no one else does
until you figure out for yourself
that it's a game
and you already know all along
and you are just looking for someone fun to play with
bellylaugh

when we empty the cupboards
just to smell the cumin
and widely eye lighter sparkles leap
and drop pennies on tin just to hear the ping
when you and I and molly are telling secrets
and I am fun to play with
you tell me that I can change the world
and believe it with the kind of faith we have
                                                in nothing

because. goddamnit.
you believe in magic.

because
sometimes we're nothing but the fastest and prettiest
110. 140. 167.
bolt of light
thunderbolts and raindrops don't spoil our graveyard picnic
when everyone thinks we might die
we know we're the only one alive

DRUGS ARE DANGEROUS KIDS / YOU'LL NEVER BE THE SAME

WHAT HAPPENS when you make friends with Molly, Lucy, Dimitri and some Fun Guys?

Molly welcomes you back to a state of pure acceptance. In your return you pass through dark and tender parts hurt in the past. Re-examining these, reopening discussion in a kind, thoughtful, gentle and loving manner, you see more dimensions to this pain and understand that you need not suffer any longer.

Truths reveal themselves. The energy surrounding us, that is us, unfolds itself. You return to simple sense joys that have been neglected too long. You see what you normally miss. You smell things you never stopped to smell. You feel air heavy on your skin. You see light separate from dark, mesmerized by its spark.

You learn of many mind pathways unexplored. You learn how deeply you can emote empathy, compassion, understanding, love. You replace the center of your consciousness with a desire to be and spread this always.

At times you are not successful. You slip back into the hard, judgment filled existence of competition, but now with have an experience upon which to re-center. You lose the fear of being vulnerable, understanding that through vulnerability comes great power. By facing truths you fear, they are unraveled and are nowhere near as dark as you imagined.

Lucy tears the veil more. You deeply settle into knowings about your past. You see the immense joy and despair inseparable in existence. You watch the mind's ability to project onto the physical world; to transform concrete into fantastic. The truth of gravity is felt within your body; the immense yogic relief of shutting off in various poses to heal your physical plane. You access a deep well of forgiveness and understanding. You process pain for which previously you had cast blame. These scars transform into a deeper understanding of decades-long interactions.

You experience the weighty sensation of being not any different from those who lived hundreds of years before. You experience the smallness of this single life and the largeness of the waterfall of humanity. You learn to look closer, but hold more loosely to what you see. To be gentle with your attention. To let subtlety reign. You see your own mortality; the decaying flesh that holds light.

Dimitri rips you from this plane of existence—with the blinders removed the full spectrum of This pours into your being. You are awestruck. You are confused. You grasp at this truth so hard to bring it back. You watch your brain/mind glitch in a loop of activity, unable to tell a start from a finish from a middle and back again. You watch your surroundings crawl with the absolute energy of life. You lay immovable while the secrets of truth and existence are poured in. Any grip on reality is torn free—unable to definitively say what is real even though you knew real from unreal just moments before. Unable to say, definitively, that you know anything to be real. Yet everything you know is real. Real. Unreal. Real. Unreal. You see the vacillation of these two states and began to live in-between.

You visit Dimitri again and you meet god dancing there. Larger than anything you've ever experienced yet as small as the invisible lens of mind. You find comfort in this vision, this idea that there is god—it's just so much bigger than anyone who ever tells you about god encourages you to see. And the diversity, multiplicity and fluidity of this Being merges inside and out.

Some Fun Guys teach you all this and more, ten-fold.

At least, you hope that is the way it goes.
You have no idea.

OKAY, CUPID

A MAN WRITES TO ASK why you have selected
other and serious about it in regards to religion.
The answer seems like it will be
important to him for some reason.

Your religion is spilled secrets of prophet pinecones,
amrita golden bees drink from desert creosotes.
One breath that splinters time.
A deep cave of silent knowing you can't quite bring back.

Everything is impermanent. Everything is absurd.
(You read this written in a bathroom stall.)

Everything is one cosmic cloth animated by the crests
and troughs of the vibration of one eternal sound.
(You probably steal that from Alan Watts.)

You use words like these to explain but he never replies.
You are either crazy or just seem that way to him.

A different stranger sends a message. And then another
to ponder whether his first note offended.
He is at least fifty percent spot on with the second
but for mostly the wrong assumptions.

How to make a narrative reply to the thoughts presented here?
You are unsure if you admire the potpourri of ideas
or are taxed by their commingling.
(Or perhaps admire the taxation of their commingling?)

Politely acknowledge acceptance,
put it down, try again later.
Outline reactions in list form,
then organize, you surmise.
Most people do not think about this
this much, you think.

You reply with a few words
and wait until tomorrow.

Tomorrow your long-time lover lays nude in the bed
with a broken right tibia smoking Sour Diesel—
your bed made altar
by the torn and frayed patchwork quilt,
the nineties neon afghan crocheted by Great Grandma Rose,
the shaggy chartreuse dinosaur (plush with wonky teeth),
a hand-looped canopy of woven yarn,
burnt orange and deep blue pashmina hanging like banners.

A drug-store-impulse-buy dreamcatcher swirls
(with synthetic feathers and lenticular eagle in flight)
gifted from the lover who sometimes joins you both in bed.

You try to write, to outline
your reflections in list form then organize.
He interrupts to talk—
about anything really—lonely as all get out
from two weeks doing nothing but
popping pharma-heroin
and growing marrow.

ASH GOOD is a narcistic millenial, poet and artist. *Years Grew a Keloid* is her first collection of words. Ash studied design and art history in Los Angeles at Loyola Marymount University and holds sacred space to invite all beings to connect with their healer and artist within. She lives in Portland, Ore.

www.ingramcontent.com/pod-product-compliance
Lightning Source LLC
Chambersburg PA
CBHW052137010526
44113CB00036B/2297